I Am a Seal

The Life of an Elephant Seal

by Darlene R. Stille illustrated by Todd Ouren

Special thanks to our advisers for their expertise:

Susan H. Shane, Ph.D., Biology
University of California at Santa Cruz

Susan Kesselring, M.A., Literacy Educator
Rosemount-Apple Valley-Eagan (Minnesota) School District

I Live in the Ocean

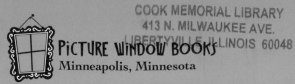

PICTURE WINDOW BOOKS
Minneapolis, Minnesota

Managing Editors: Bob Temple, Catherine Neitge
Creative Director: Terri Foley
Editors: Nadia Higgins, Patricia Stockland
Editorial Adviser: Andrea Cascardi
Designer: Todd Ouren
Page production: Picture Window Books
The illustrations in this book were prepared digitally.

Picture Window Books
5115 Excelsior Boulevard
Suite 232
Minneapolis, MN 55416
877-845-8392
www.picturewindowbooks.com

Printed in the United States of America.

Library of Congress Cataloging-in-Publication Data
Stille, Darlene R.
I am a seal : the life of an elephant seal /
by Darlene R. Stille ; illustrated by Todd Ouren.
p. cm. — (I live in the ocean)
Includes bibliographical references (p.   ).
ISBN 1-4048-0598-2 (reinforced lib. bdg.)
1. Elephant seals—Juvenile literature. I. Ouren, Todd, ill.
II. Title.

QL737.P64S73 2004
599.79'4—dc22   2004000889

I am a seal. Watch me swim and dive in the water. Watch me wriggle my body over the rocky beach.

Bbbrrruuummm! Listen to me rumble. Look at my long nose. No wonder they call me an elephant seal.

All seals are good divers, but I am the diving champ! I take a deep breath. Then down, down, down I go. I can stay under water for more than an hour.

Look at how fast I can swim. I swish my back flippers from side to side, just like a fish flips its tail. I use my front flippers to steer. *Whooooosh!*

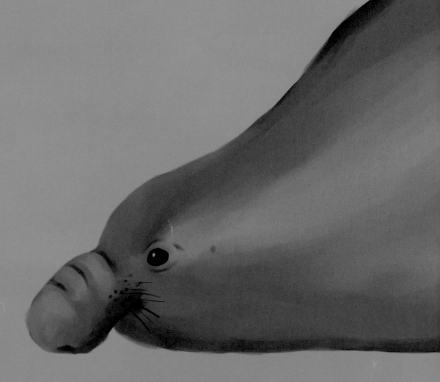

4

Elephant seals can dive 1 mile
(1 1/2 kilometers) deep.

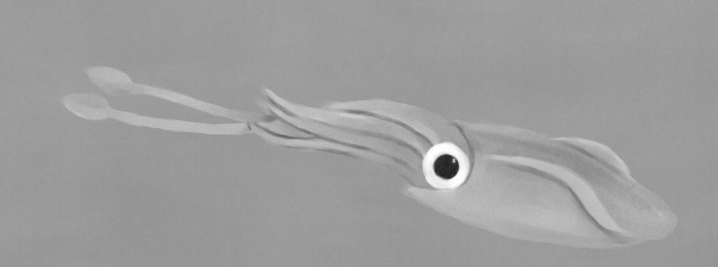

Seals eat all kinds
of sea animals, including
fish, crabs, shrimp, rays,
and even small sharks.
Great white sharks and
killer whales eat seals.

It's dark and quiet down here in the deep water.
I use my big eyes and good ears to hunt for food.
Here comes a squid. *Yum!*

I use my sharp teeth to hold my prey.
Then I swallow it whole.

I don't have any trouble finding food. I eat and
eat until big rolls of blubber hang from my neck.
My blubber is fat that acts like a blanket.
It keeps me warm in the chilly water.

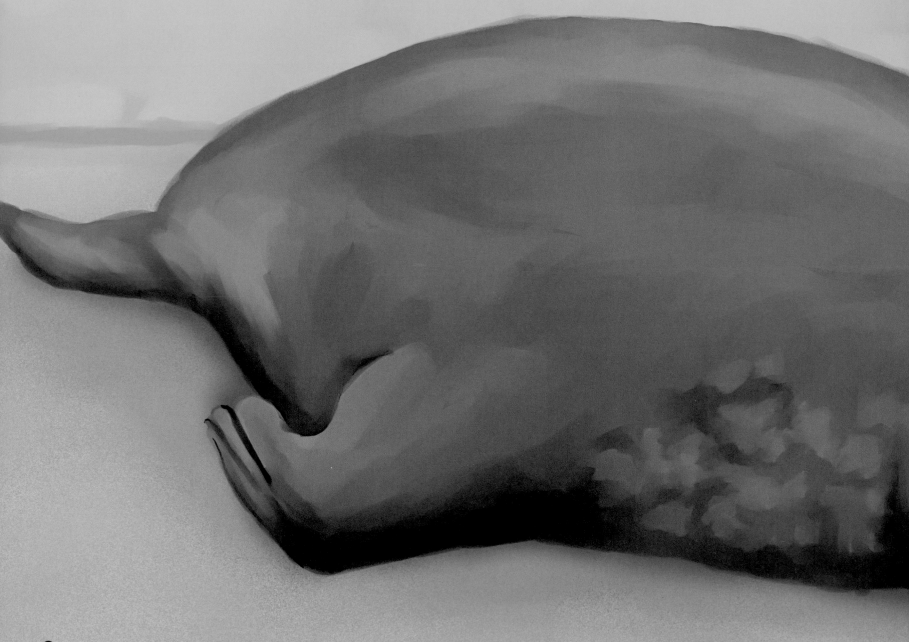

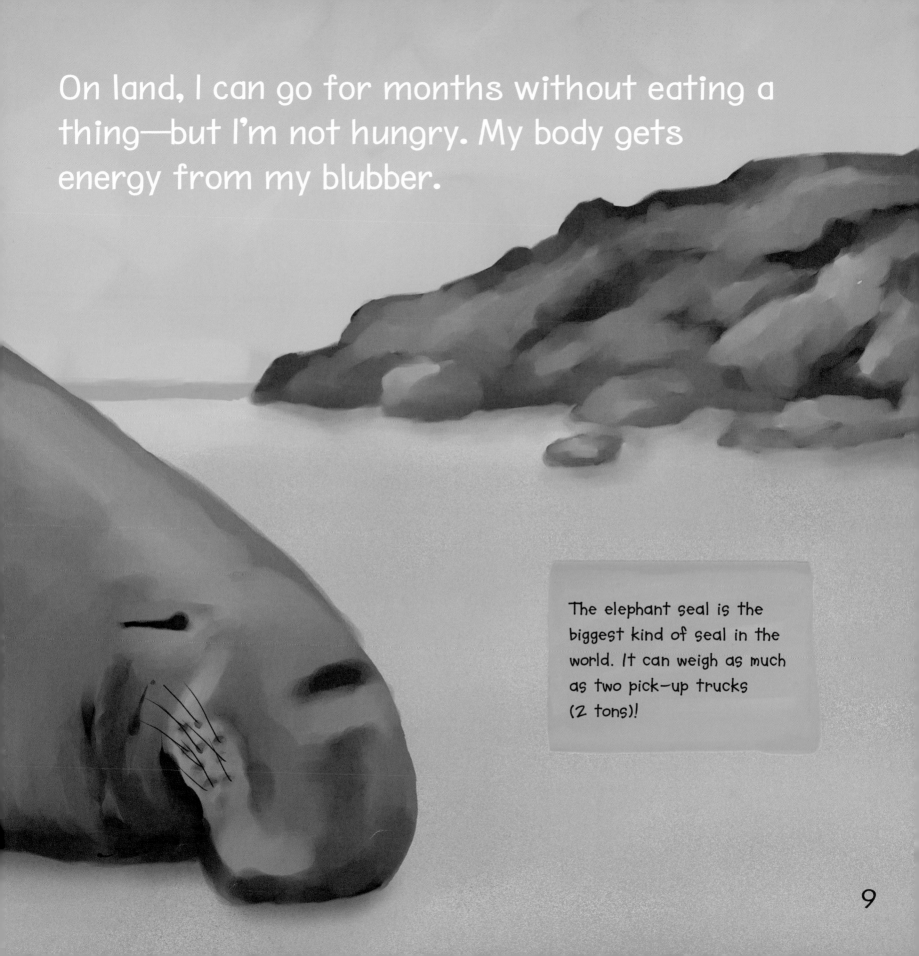

On land, I can go for months without eating a thing—but I'm not hungry. My body gets energy from my blubber.

The elephant seal is the biggest kind of seal in the world. It can weigh as much as two pick-up trucks (2 tons)!

9

Have you ever seen me and my friends lying together on a beach? People driving by stop their cars to look at us. As many as 10,000 of us crowd together on my beach in California.

Do you notice anything funny about some of these other seals? They don't have long noses! Only grown-up males have noses like mine.

A male elephant seal uses his nose to show other males who's boss. The special nose makes a loud noise. That noise tells other male seals to back off.

This beach is where we were all born. It's called a rookery. We only stay here in the summer and winter, though. Sometimes, to find the best food, I leave and swim all the way to Alaska.

In summer, I come here to molt. That's when all my fur rubs off. I relax on the beach for a whole month while my new fur grows in.

Elephant seals travel farther than any other mammal. They swim about 13,000 miles (20,800 kilometers) a year on their trips.

In winter, we come back here to have babies. Look at their shiny black fur. Listen to them squawk. *Awrrkk.*

Each pup's noise is different. Mothers listen for their baby's special sound. That's how the mothers keep track of their babies on the crowded beach.

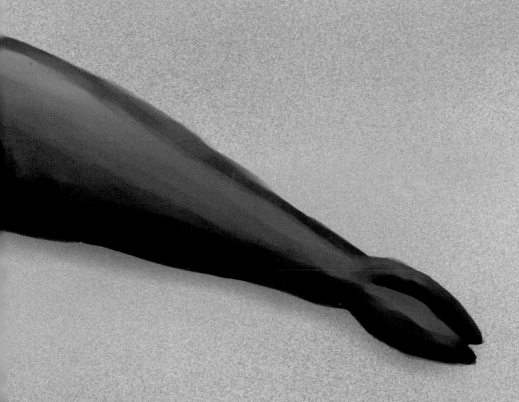

Each mother has her own call, too. A pup listens for and follows its mother's sound.

When I was a pup, I could call out to my mother a few minutes after I was born. I stuck close by her side. My mother took good care of me. She fed me her rich milk. I got bigger and bigger.

A mother seal usually gives birth to one pup at a time. At birth, a pup is about 70 pounds (32 kilograms). Within one month, it gains about 200 pounds (90 kilograms)!

When I was a month old, my mother left. She knew it was time for me to start growing up.

I stayed at the rookery for another month or so. I lived with the other young seals. We learned to swim in the waves close to shore.

After its mother leaves, a young seal is called a weaner. Weaners don't eat anything during the time they live without their mothers at the rookery. They live off their blubber.

19

I learned to swim farther and farther. One day I swam away. I was ready to explore the ocean. Now I dive, swim, and play in the water all day.

When elephant seals are at sea, they spend almost all of their time under the water. They can even sleep under water while they hold their breath.

21

Look Closely at an Elephant Seal

You can tell this elephant seal is a grown-up male by his long nose.

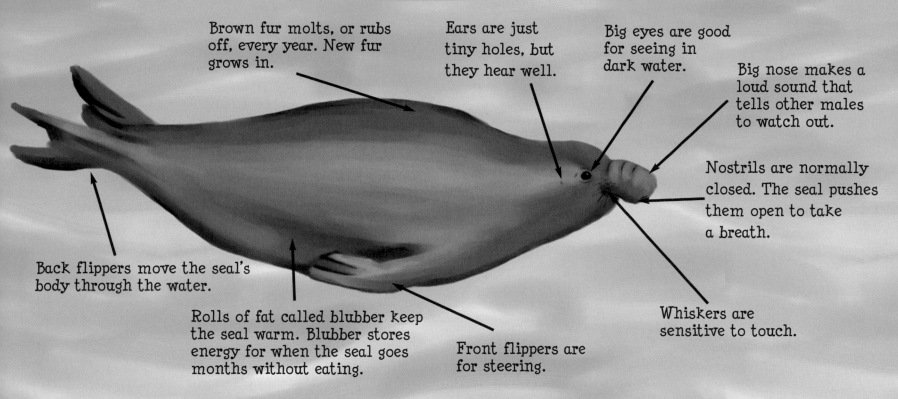

Brown fur molts, or rubs off, every year. New fur grows in.

Ears are just tiny holes, but they hear well.

Big eyes are good for seeing in dark water.

Big nose makes a loud sound that tells other males to watch out.

Nostrils are normally closed. The seal pushes them open to take a breath.

Back flippers move the seal's body through the water.

Rolls of fat called blubber keep the seal warm. Blubber stores energy for when the seal goes months without eating.

Front flippers are for steering.

Whiskers are sensitive to touch.

Fun Facts

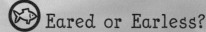 Eared or Earless?

There are 34 species (or kinds) of seals. Scientists divide these seals into two main groups: eared seals and earless seals. Eared seals, such as sea lions and fur seals, have little flaps for ears. Earless seals, such as elephant seals, have tiny holes for ears. No matter what their ears look like, all seals have good hearing.

Packing on the Pounds

A baby hooded seal drinks milk from its mother for only four days. The milk is very rich. During those four days, the baby gains about 60 pounds (27 kilograms), doubling its birth weight.

No Ordinary Teeth

A walrus is the only kind of seal with two long front teeth, called tusks. A walrus uses its tusks to defend itself from polar bears. It also uses them like hooks. It sticks them into land or ice and then pulls its body out of the water.

Not-So-Fun Fact

Seals face dangers caused by people. Seals can get tangled in fishing nets or plastic straps used on ships to tie boxes. In some places, people hunt seals for their fine fur and their meat. Some countries have laws to protect seals from these dangers.

A Little One

The ringed seal is one of the smallest seals. It is about 3 1/2 feet (1 meter) long and weighs between 100 and 200 pounds (45 and 90 kilograms).

The Speediest

Sea lions are the fastest seals. They can swim up to 25 miles (40 kilometers) per hour. That's about as fast as a car on a city street.

Sea Bears...

Seals were once called sea bears. When Europeans first saw seals, they thought the animals looked like bears.

...Or Sea Dogs?

The California sea lion makes a sound like a dog's bark.

Icy Roofs

Some earless seals live in cold water under big sheets of ice. They use their sharp teeth and claws to make holes in the ice. They can breathe through these holes.

Glossary

blubber—a thick layer of fat under the skin of seals and other mammals that live in the ocean; blubber keeps the animals warm

molt—shedding fur, feathers, or an outer layer of skin; after molting, a new covering grows

prey—an animal that is hunted and eaten by another animal

rookery—the place where seals crowd together to molt and to have babies

To Learn More

At the Library

Hollenbeck, Kathleen M. *Islands of Ice: The Story of a Harp Seal.* Norwalk, Conn.: Soundprints, 2001.

Rustad, Martha E. H. *Seals.* Mankato, Minn.: Pebble Books, 2001.

Stewart, Melissa. *Seals, Sea Lions, and Walruses.* New York: Franklin Watts, 2001.

On the Web

FactHound offers a safe, fun way to find Web sites related to this book.
All of the sites on FactHound have been researched by our staff.
www.facthound.com

1. Visit the FactHound home page.
2. Enter a search word related to this book, or type in this special code: 1404805982.
3. Click the FETCH IT button.

Your trusty FactHound will fetch the best Web sites for you!

Index

Look for all the books in this series:

I Am a Dolphin
The Life of a Bottlenose Dolphin

I Am a Sea Turtle
The Life of a Green Sea Turtle

I Am a Shark
The Life of a Hammerhead Shark

I Am a Fish
The Life of a Clown Fish

I Am a Seal
The Life of an Elephant Seal

I Am a Whale
The Life of a Humpback Whale